Manna from Heaven

Books available from:

USA   Alan Ames Ministry
                         PO Box 200
                         233 Glasgow Avenue SW
                         Kellogg
                         Minnesota 55945
Phone: 507 767 3027

Australia   Touch of heaven
                         (Alan Ames Ministry)
                         PO Box 85
                         Wembley, 6014
                         West Australia
Phone: 61 89275 6608
Fax: 61 89382 4392
Web: http://www.alanames.ws

Email: alan@alanames.ws

The decree of the Congregation of the Propagation of the Faith, A.A.S 58, 1186 (approved by Pope Paul VI on October 14, 1966) states that the Nihil Obstat and Imprimatur are no longer required on publications that deal with private revelations, provided that they contain nothing contrary to faith and morals.

The publisher recognizes and accepts that the final authority regarding the events described in this book rests with the Holy See of Rome, to whose judgement we willingly submit.

4.

This book is dedicated to Msgr. Peter Dunne who has always shown me a compassionate and generous heart.

Books and Tapes available by C.A.Ames

Title	Price US$
Through the Eyes of Jesus, Trilogy	26.00
Through the Eyes of Jesus, Vol 1	8.00
Through the Eyes of Jesus, Vol 2	8.00
Through the Eyes of Jesus, Vol 3	8.00
Heaven Speaks	10.00
Messages to Carver Alan Ames	10.00
Our Father Speaks	12.00
Stories of Love	11.00
The Way of Hope	8.00
Salaam Shalom	10.00
Our Mother's Heart	10.00
What is Truth	8.00
Brought to Life	11.00

Videos, Audios & Rosary available by C.A.Ames

Through His Eyes, Focus Video 1	20.00
Revelations from Heaven, Focus Video 2	20.00
Touching Lives, Touching Souls, Focus Video	20.00
Three Focus Videos	50.00
Come Back to God, Video	20.00
Why God? Vol 1, Video	15.00
Why God? Vol 2, Video	15.00
Why God? Both videos	25.00
Audio Tape	3.00
Eucharistic Rosary Package (Including Rosary Beads)	3.00

INTRODUCTION

After The Lord came and changed my life for the better and invited me to live close to Him, He explained, first through the saints and Our Blessed Mother and then Himself, that if I wanted to be truly close to Him, it is possible, by living a Eucharistic life.

At first I did not understand what was meant to being truly close to Him but later, through His Divine grace in the Eucharist, I began to understand a little. I was given many messages and insights about the Eucharist which helped open not only my eyes, but my very soul to the Lord, and because of the great graces I received from these messages, I put them together in this book in the hope that all who read it will also receive these graces.

Every word that has been given to me about the Eucharist emphasizes the great love God has for mankind. A love so enormous that in the Eucharist God comes to mankind and offers Himself over and over. In every Eucharist Our Lord Jesus calls out to each one from His Divine heart 'Here I am. Come to me and be loved.'

This Divine offering truly is the greatest gift God gives to mankind, for it is the gift of Himself coming into mere mortals so that every person who receives Him can find their true selves, their true lives and their true love. It is in this gift that God opens His Divine Self to mankind as an opening of the doorway to heaven. As that door opens the heavenly glory, love and joy pours out into each person. Then if each one in turn opens themselves to God in this the greatest of the sacraments, that heavenly grace fills the entire being, mind, body and soul, and lifts the person high into God's heart.

Once I experienced this lifting of my entire being into God's heart, I knew in that moment life without this most wonderful union was empty. I knew then what Our Lord, Jesus meant when He said, *(Jesus said to them 'Amen, amen, I say to you unless you eat the flesh of the son of man and drink his blood you do not have life within you' John 6:53).* Now with Our Lord filling my entire self with His Divine Self I knew God loved me and I knew that I loved Him and I never wanted to be away from Him again. As I united with Him I saw that life from now on could be so different than before because now I knew God was with me and that He in His divine love would take care of me, guide me, nourish me and change my life for the better.

I started to understand that God is goodness and that all good comes from Him, that there is no bad in Him and that if I accepted His goodness into my life then my life would be filled with good and with happiness. I wondered why in the past I had some fear of God for now I knew there is nothing to fear from The One who is eternal love. This union was showing me some of the truth of God's love and now I knew I wanted that truth always with me. It became obvious that if I wanted to keep this joy, this love, this happiness, this excitement in my life I must keep close to where it comes from and so I must keep close to God.

I had the desire to go to frequent Eucharist because without the daily union with Our Lord there is an emptiness, yes, even a hurt inside of me as my entire being cries out for what it knows is best for it. Also in this blessed union with God came a change deep inside me, a change I liked and wanted to continue. I began to think of love more, love of God and love of others. This of course is what happens when a person unites frequently with God *(Beloved, let us love one another, because love is of God; everyone who loves is begotten by God and knows God. 1 John 4:7)* the person becomes more and more like God, becomes an image of God. Which is of course what we were created to be *(God created man in his image. Genesis 1:27).* It is part of the wonderful gift God gives mankind in the Eucharist, the opportunity to change to be like the Divine Lord but not the same, still to be human but to take on the characteristics of the Divine loving Heart of Jesus as we unite and exist in the Eucharistic love of God.

I found that by coming to the Eucharist and seeking to be changed by the Lord and by asking Him in every Eucharist to change me, He began to do so. It has been a long and continuous process, which will never end as I need to be changed every day and I need to be brought to life in Him every day. It is a process all who receive Our Lord in communion should be undergoing if they want to live the way of God. His way of course is the way of love, and that is why it becomes normal that when a person is Eucharistic they change to be more loving and be more like Christ, Our lord *(God is love, and whoever remains in love remains in God and God in him. 1 John 4:16).*

It is important however, as I have learned, that when one comes to the Eucharist they must be prepared to give themselves totally to God. It is with this giving of self that the soul can be truly opened to receive God as one should. It is with this commitment of a person's entire life, entire being to Christ, Our Lord in the Holy Eucharist, that the person, with their free will and by the grace of God, puts themselves aside and in humble love and worship of the Lord opens their innermost self to the heavenly food of God Himself. As they are opened in this way God pours out in abundance His Divine grace and lifts the person to experience the most intimate of unions possible, the union of God and man.

It is also in this union that a person, as they offer themselves to God, in God, with God, and by God, is drawn into a deeper relationship with The Holy Trinity. Through this union a person can unite in the suffering of Christ, Our Lord on the cross by offering all the suffering they have had, may still have, and may have in the future, to God in thanks for His love shown through and in His Son Jesus. So that their suffering now becomes part of the sacrificial offering of Jesus in the Holy Mass and as part of that holy offering is taken deep into the heart of the Father by the power of the Holy Spirit.

It is when this happens the person becomes the vessel of grace they are meant to be, for now the Holy Spirit fills the person with divine grace so that the love of Christ, Our Lord can be truly seen in the person. Then through that love, the graces and gifts of the Holy Spirit can be magnified and taken out to the world to be shared with others as it is meant to be. As the person does this they will find, as I have, that they are opened, through the sharing with others, of God's love, opened even more to God. They will find that this act of service to God and to fellow man brings one to another level of being Christ-like for now a person serves as Our Lord served.

As this is experienced not only is the human sight opened but also the spiritual sight and one starts to see life in a different way. It becomes obvious that without the Eucharist at the centre of a life, life is empty.

It becomes obvious that if a person wants to live in Christ's way then the person must live in Christ and to live in Him is to live in the Eucharist. It becomes obvious that it is imperative to follow the command that Our Lord gave at the Last Supper (*'Do this in memory of me'. Luke 22:19)* if one is to live the faith that Our Lord gave to us.

It is seen that not to live the Eucharistic life is to deny The Lord and to live an empty faith because the Eucharist is the foundation of the faith, as it is Christ Himself. It becomes clear that fullness of faith can only be found in and through the Eucharist, as in living the Eucharistic faith a person is drawn to all the sacraments and to see the beauty, grace and divine love in each one. No wonder this most sacred gift, this, the Sacrament of Sacraments comes under so much attack. If doubt and disbelief can be sown in the hearts of God's people about the Eucharist, then that is doubt and disbelief in Christ Himself and what He gave to us and also it can become a denial of faith. (*'O you of little faith, why did you doubt?' Matthew 14:31).* If doubt and disbelief can be sown into hearts then the seeds for division are planted, seeds which, when they grow, bring disunity among the people of God and no longer are all part of the one true Eucharistic church given by God, but become part of churches created by man in the weakness of pride. (*As a result of this many of his disciples returned to their former way of life and no longer accompanied him. John 6:66).*

The Eucharist calls all people to union in God and into unity in their love of Him and each other. So that in Our Eucharistic Lord's presence we can all be one in Him, one in His body as the holy people, the holy church He established in love to reign eternal with Him in His glory.

As you read the messages, you will see some have scriptural references, while others have none. This is because in the beginning the Lord did not give me any references, but from December 1995 the Lord began to do so at various times. When I am given the references from Holy Scripture, it may be one or two lines, or only one or two words from a line. Sometimes two or three lines from different parts of Holy Scripture are combined to make the reference. The references at first were taken either from the Jerusalem or Douay-Rheims Bibles, but later to avoid any confusion, my spiritual director and I decided to use only the New American Bible for references.

I pray that all who read this book will be drawn into the Holy Words of Our Lord and to see what He gave to mankind in the giving of Himself and what He continues to give to mankind in the perpetual sacrifice. That those who eat of His divine body and drink of His divine blood have their souls satisfied in this, the greatest union of love. That each one will come to know and appreciate that the true manna from heaven is Our Lord, Jesus Christ in every Holy Eucharist celebrated by His one holy and apostolic church.

God bless,

Alan Ames

18/06/95 Jesus
Bread and wine, body and blood,
Bread and wine, fruit of love,
Bread and wine, I am the Lord.

03/07/95 Jesus
My body and blood lead to heaven,
My body and blood lead to eternal joy,
My body and blood lead to The Father.
The Eucharist, My body and blood, My gift to mankind.

04/07/95 Jesus
Filled with love, filled with truth,
Filled with God when you receive My body.

Filled with hope, filled with joy,
Filled with God when you receive My body.

Filled with charity, filled with faith,
Filled with God when you receive My body.

The more you receive My body, the more you are filled
and the more you have to share.

08/07/95 Jesus
Truth of truths, I am in the host.
Love of loves, I am in the host.
God of God, I am in the host...
The truth and the love of God are to be found in the
host.

08/07/95 Jesus
Find peace in My body,
Find comfort in My heart,
Find love in My soul,
Find it all in the Eucharist.

19/07/95 Jesus
When you take My body within
you take My whole being within.

When you take My body within
you take My spirit within.

When you take My body within
you take My truth within.

I am the truth that brings your spirit into being.

02/09/95 Jesus
Find peace within the Eucharist,
Find joy within the Eucharist,
Find hope within the Eucharist,
The Eucharist...Food of life, food of love, food of God.

03/09/95 Father
Take My love within,
Take My joy within,
Take My hope within,
Do this when you receive My Son in the Eucharist.

07/09/95 Jesus
To receive Me within is to be filled with My love, a love you can bring to others, a love you can share with others, and a love you can fill others with. The love of God, there for all and all there from it.

12/09/95 Jesus
On an altar lies the sacrifice that forgave mankind,
On an altar lies the sacrifice that is often forgotten,
On an altar lies the sacrifice of My body and blood in the Sacrament of the most Holy Eucharist.
A Sacrament that should not be forgotten,
A Sacrament of love, a love that forgives all.

15/09/95 Jesus
To join in love with Me is to become one in God's love.
This is the truth of communion.

18/09/95 Jesus
United in love,
United in joy,
United in eternity…Through the Eucharist.

20/09/95 Mother
Finding the joy of Jesus,
Finding the love of Jesus,
Finding Jesus in the Eucharist.

28/09/95 Father
Find peace in My Son's heart,
Find love in My Son's presence,
Find truth in My Son's body,
All found in the Eucharist,
All found in the bread of life,
All found in Jesus My Son.

04/10/95 Father
Take My Son within and become one in love, one in spirit and one in heart.

09/10/95 Father
Aroma of love - breath of Jesus,
Taste of love - body of Jesus,
Sweetness of love - blood of Jesus.
Jesus, who has the sweetest love to share with all, a love that fills the heart with the most fragrant perfume. A love once tasted always desired.

09/10/95 Jesus
To feed your soul, come to Me,
To nurture your love, come to Me,
To grow within your spirit, come to Me.
Come to me and I will feed you with My body and blood which will nurture your spirit and help it to grow in My love.

Matthew 11:28 Come to me all who you who labour and are burdened.

10/10/95 Jesus
Receiving My body is receiving My love.
Once you have received, share My love with all, for it is in the
giving that you receive as you should.

13/10/95 Jesus
Find peace within the Eucharist, the peace that brings the strength of God into your heart.

31/10/95 Father
Pure love in the Eucharist,
True love in the Eucharist,
Love...God, Who is love... in the Eucharist.

31/10/95 Jesus
Find My love in the bread of life,
Find your faith through the bread of life,
Find your faith strengthened by My love in the bread of life.

12/11/95 Jesus
Friends share a meal,
Friends share a drink,
Friends share a life.
Share with Me your life and find your strength in My body and blood.

2011/95 Father
Find the peace that comes from being one with God by uniting with My Son Jesus in the Eucharist.

26/11/95 Jesus
Think of My love and you are filled with it.
Think of Me and you are one with Me.
Think of God when you receive My love in the
Eucharist and be filled with Me.

12/12/95 Jesus
Find in the bread of life the strength you need to carry
on.
Find in the bread of life the love you have to share.
Find in the bread of life the peace you want for your
soul.
I am the bread of life...Find it all in Me.

14/12/95 Jesus
In My body find My love,
In My love find Me.

16/12/95 Jesus
Eat of Me and find peace,
Eat of Me and find strength,
Eat of Me and find love.
In the Eucharist the peaceful love of God that fills you
with strength is to be found.

17/12/95 Jesus
The joy you feel within when you receive My body and
blood is the joy I share with you. It is a joy I long to
share with all.

18.

28/12/95 Jesus
To join in love with Me is a special gift I offer all mankind.
It is a gift that is often underestimated or not accepted as true.
It is a gift that can save so many.
Encourage My children to increase the receiving of My body and blood and then see My church grow in the strength of God's love.

06/01/96 Jesus
Flesh of My flesh,
Blood of My blood,
Truth of My truth…
The Eucharist.

04/02/96 Jesus
The Eucharist - a celebration,
The Eucharist - a joy,
The Eucharist - My love.

17/02/96 Jesus
In the bread - My body,
In the wine - My blood,
In mankind - doubts.

John 4:10 If you only knew what God is offering.

19/02/96 Jesus
To eat of Me is to unite with Me,
To drink of Me is to enter My heart,
To unite with Me in the Eucharist is to fill yourself with My love and to fill yourself with My love shows your love of Me.

13/03/96 Jesus
A heart unites with Me when a person receives My body and blood.

A heart unites with Me when a person believes in My body and blood.

A heart unites with Me when a person believes that My body and blood is received in the Sacrament of Communion and they take Me within in love.

John 6:47 I tell you most solemnly everybody who believes
John 6:48 I am the bread of life.

19/03/96 Jesus
As the bread that is My body is taken within, the person receiving Me becomes one in My love.
As the bread that is My body becomes part of that person, we unite in joy, the joy that is God.
As the bread that is My body fills the very spirit of the person, they join with Me to become a light in the dark.

19/03/96 Jesus
My body and blood bring you everything if only you believe.

29/04/96 Jesus
In the Mass, My body, My blood.
In the Mass, My love, My joy.
In the Mass, Me.

John 17:19 For their sake I consecrate myself so that they too may be consecrated in truth.

02/05/96 Father
In the Mass see My Son's sacrifice.
In the Mass see My Son's gift.
In the Mass see My Son Jesus.

Psalms 94:6 Come let us adore and fall down; and weep before the Lord.

14/05/96 Father
Drinking from the cup of love means to share this love.
Eating of the bread of forgiveness means to offer this forgiveness to all.
Uniting with My Son Jesus through His body and blood in the Eucharist fills you with God's love and forgiveness that I long all to share with you.

20/05/96 Father

In the bread of life find Jesus. In Jesus find life.
In the wine of forgiveness find Jesus. In Jesus find forgiveness.
In the bread and wine of communion find Jesus' forgiving love which brings true life.

Luke 18:30 In the world to come, eternal life.

25/05/96 Father

To refresh yourself, wash yourself in My Son's precious blood.
To feed your spirit, eat of My Son's body.
To find peace in your heart, become one with My Son Jesus in communion.

28/05/96 Mother

In the food of life you find my Son Jesus, for He is life.
In the wine of love you see Jesus, for He is love.
In the sustenance that saves you, know Jesus, for He is the saviour.
Jesus brings true life to all.
Jesus offers salvation to all.
Jesus Who is love for all.

18/06/96 Jesus

When you unite with Me in the Most Holy Sacrament of Communion you are engulfed in My love, in My peace, and in My joy.
Like a ship in the ocean, if you go with the flow of the water your ride will be much smoother than if you sail against it. Accept My love and let Me lead you. Do not resist or you become like the ship struggling against the tide.

07/07/96 Father
In hope, receive My Son's body.
In love, receive My Son's blood.
In union with My Son Jesus bring My love to those who
search without hope.
My love is Jesus and Jesus is the only hope, bring Jesus
to all.

07/07/96 Jesus
In love united,
In the sacrament joined,
In the sacrament of love that is My body and blood we
unite to become joined forevermore.

*Jeremiah 50:5 'Come,' they say, 'let us bind ourselves
to Yahweh by an everlasting covenant never to be
forgotten.'*

13/07/96 Jesus
In the bread and wine...I am.
In the Eucharist...I am.
In the sacrifice for forgiveness...I am.
I am and perpetually I will be.

14/07/96 Jesus
One body, one blood, one God...The Eucharist.

31/07/96 Jesus
Blood and wine,
Body and bread,
God and love.

05/08/96 Father
In the Mass find love,
In the Mass find peace,
In the Mass find hope,
For Jesus brings His love to you in the Eucharist, which,
if you accept it, will bring you peace of heart and hope
in life.

13/08/96 Father
The bread of life is offered to mankind in every
Eucharist.
The blood of salvation is offered to mankind in every
Sacrament of Communion.
The food of eternal joy is offered to mankind in every
celebration of love in the Mass.
Eat of My Son Jesus and be filled with love.
Drink of My Son Jesus and be washed in joy.
Unite with My Son Jesus and live forever.

14/08/96 Jesus
In the bread of communion I am.
In the wine of communion I am.
In those who receive My body and blood I am.

A joyful gift that I offer to all.
A mystery of God that many doubt.
A wonderful union of love that is a true mystery of God
that none should doubt.

Luke 11:3 Give us each day our daily bread.

12/09/96 Jesus
Food of life,
Food for all,
Food of eternal life that is for all...
My body and My blood.

Proverbs 8:35 For the man who finds me finds life, he will win favour from Yahweh.

20/10/96 Jesus
To receive My body and blood is the greatest gift you can receive from Me, for when you do this I become one with you and you become one with Me.

In this union of God and man the spirit can be strengthened and brought closer to Me.

In this union of divinity and humanity the spirit can be filled with the love of God, divine love.

In this union of the Son of God and God's children the spirit unites to become one family of God's merciful love.

So much in the sacrament, there for all mankind, if in humble love, they will accept the truth.

Acts 17:28 In him we live and move and have our being.

01/11/96 St Gregory
In the bread of heaven lies eternity,
In the blood of heaven, forgiveness.

03/11/96 Jesus
In the Mass, the living sacrifice.
In the Mass, the salvation of mankind.
In the Mass, the perpetual offer of My love.

05/11/96 Mother
Open your heart in the Mass and be filled with the Holy
Spirit.

25/11/96 Jesus
My love is in you,
My graces fill you,
My heart is yours,
When you unite in the Eucharist with Me.

08/12/96 Jesus
Celebration of love, Sacrifice of love, Offer of love...
The Eucharist.

Psalms 108:4 Your love is high as heaven.

09/12/96 Jesus
Joined in love,
United with Me,
Filled with God...
In the Eucharist.

Matthew 28:7 It is there you will see him.

26.

14/12/96 Jesus
Accepting Me within in the Eucharist, is welcoming My
embrace of love.
Accepting Me within in the Eucharist, is joining in My
love.
Accepting Me within in the Eucharist, is love.

Matthew 13:23 The one who received.

23/12/96 Jesus
A gentleness of heart,
A peace of mind,
A strength of spirit…
All found in the Eucharist.

Psalms 119:45 I shall walk in all freedom.

26/12/96 St Stephen
In the bread of life is eternity,
In the bread of life is love,
In the bread of life is the promise of Jesus.

Psalms 77:3 I thought of God and sighed.

09/02/97 Jesus
My body and blood has within it all that mankind needs
to live and all that mankind needs to love.

Isaiah 6:3 Holy, holy, holy is the Lord of Hosts.

08/03/97 Jesus
Be at peace in Me,
Be at ease in Me,
Be at one in Me
Be with Me in the Eucharist

Job 11:8 It is higher than the heavens

15/03/97 Jesus
In My body is love, in My blood, forgiveness.

Proverbs 6:21 Bind them ever to your heart.

20/03/97 Jesus
On the altar I place My body and blood as an offering of love.
On the altar I offer Myself perpetually in love.
On the altar I place the answer to all of mankind's needs.
I place Myself before mankind and offer the way to true happiness and true love.
Accept My offering and become part of it when you unite with Me in the Eucharist.

22/03/97 Mother
The food of life is love.
Jesus is love and He is found in the Eucharist, which is the food of life.

28.

26/03/97 Jesus
The bread and the wine.
My body and the cross.
My Spirit and The Father.

When you eat of My body and blood in the Eucharist you unite with My suffering on the cross and open your soul to My Father and My Spirit.

Job 16:19 Hence forth I have a witness in heaven.

01/04/97 Jesus
My heart, My soul, My Divinity, My body, My blood...
The Eucharist.

Ezekiel 39:21 That is how I shall display my glory to the nations.

17/04/97 Jesus
In My body is salvation.
In My blood, eternity.

Psalms 132:14 Here I dwell for that is my desire.

17/04/97 Holy Spirit
Our Father in heaven unites us in His love. I AM that love.
Our Father in heaven fills us with His Spirit. I AM that Spirit.
Our Father in heaven is one within us. I AM within you.
With the Father I am, as love I am, and in the Spirit I am.
When you unite with Jesus in the bread of life you become united with the Trinity of God.

Luke 24:48 Now you shall be witnesses to this.

27/04/97 Jesus
Be at one with Me in My love,
Be at one with Me in My mercy,
Be at one with Me in the Eucharist.

29/04/97 Jesus
In the bread find life,
In the blood find love,
In the Eucharist find Me.

Wisdom 6:3 A gift to you from the Lord.

02/06/97 Jesus
The body of love. The blood of forgiveness.
The Eucharist - My body and My blood.

05/06/97 Mother
In the heart of a priest should be the love of Jesus in the
Eucharist. If it is not how can he be a priest?

13/06/97 Holy Spirit
In union with Jesus is in union with me.
In union with Jesus is in union with the Father.
In union with Jesus is in union with God.

Romans 1:25 Who is blessed forever.

15/06/97 Mother
The lamb of God,
The sacrificial lamb.

The lamb of love,
The forgiving lamb.

The lamb of hope,
The giving lamb.

This is Jesus in every Eucharist.

Job 25:2 What sovereignty, what awe, is his who keeps the peace in his heights.

17/06/97 Jesus
Surrounded by love,
Surrounded by peace,
Surrounded by Me,
When you accept My truth in the Eucharist.

John 7:28 So you know me.

20/06/97 Jesus
My body and blood in the Eucharist become so by the power of the Holy Spirit in the priest.
My body and blood in the Eucharist are the gift I give perpetually through the priests.
My body and blood in the Eucharist are there through the priests and none other.

Luke 9:16 And looking up to heaven, he said the blessing over them.

27/06/97 Jesus
Placing the Eucharist in the centre of your life brings true life and true peace.

Hosea 10:1 Yielding plenty of fruit.

06/07/97 Mother
The Eucharist...A gift from God of God.

Psalms 73:1 How good God is.

24/07/97 Jesus
In the presence of love evil flees.
In the presence of love peace exists.
In the presence of love life becomes a joy.
I am love and I am present in the bread and wine of communion.

Psalms 67:8 That the ends of the earth may revere our God.

02/08/97 Jesus
At exposition I open My heart to those who are there and fill their lives with graces.

04/08/97 Jesus
Bread and wine, love divine.
Bread and wine can make you Mine.
Bread and wine, the truth throughout time.

Bread and wine, divinity,
Bread and wine, unity,
Bread and wine, eternity.

32.

Bread and wine, I am,
Bread and wine, We can be one,
Bread and wine, Forever.

10/08/97 Mother
Be filled with peace,
Be filled with joy,
Be filled with God,
In the Eucharist.

Be filled with love,
Be filled with hope,
Be filled with divinity,
In the Eucharist.

Be filled with truth,
Be filled with eternity,
Be filled with Jesus,
In the Eucharist.

Zechariah 8:4 The Lord of hosts.

18/08/97 Jesus
In the bread of life you will find true meaning if you believe.
In the bread of life you will find the reason for living if you have faith.
In the bread of life you will find heaven awaiting if you trust.
I am the bread of life and all those who believe this will find heaven awaiting and will find their faith and trust in My body and blood has opened the door to heaven for them.

John 12:44 Whoever believes in me.

25/08/97 Father
With the Eucharist as the centre of your life, life becomes a celebration of love, life becomes a joy and life becomes what it is supposed to be...Holy.

Ezekiel 20:12 The Lord who made them holy.

31/08/97 Jesus
I am the bread of life and I am offered to everyone in the Eucharist as the food of heaven that brings eternal joy.

Daniel 1:3 Of royal blood.

06/09/97 Jesus
In your heart find peace,
In your heart find hope,
In your heart find love,
Each time you receive Me in the Eucharist.

Baruch 4:22 The eternal God.

14/09/97 Mother
Be at peace in God,
Be one with God,
Be joined to God,
In the Eucharist.

Esther 9:11 In the stronghold
Ezekiel 1:3 Of the Lord.

15/09/97 Mother
The Lord awaits in the Eucharist to fill you with His love and to make you complete in Him.

1Corinthians 2:9 What God has prepared for those who love him.

17/09/97 Jesus
In the Eucharist I open My heart and offer My love to all.
They only need to open their hearts and accept Me within to receive that love.

Acts 10:23 He invited them in.

21/10/97 Jesus
In the Eucharist are mankind's needs fulfilled.
In the Eucharist are mankind's desires satisfied.
In the Eucharist are mankind's souls fed eternally.
For I am the Eucharist.

Matthew 26:64 The Son of man.
Luke 7:36 Dine with him.

29/10/97 Jesus
Sink into My love within the Eucharist by opening your heart to Me and allowing your spirit to unite with Mine.
Then find united in My love anything is possible.

Psalms 37:4 Find your delight in the Lord who will give you your heart's desire.

02/11/97 Mother
In the Eucharist find all you need to do God's work…
Find God.

08/11/97 Father
Be aware of Jesus in your life by receiving Him in the Eucharist each day, for in the Eucharist I give you your daily bread.

Ephesians 5:32 This is a great mystery.

16/11/97 Mother
In the Eucharist, my Son.
In the Eucharist, our God.
In the Eucharist...Eternity.

Psalms 14:1 Fools say in their hearts, 'there is no God.'

18/11/97 Father
The bread of life, Jesus.
The wine of salvation, Jesus.
The Son of God, Jesus.
There is no other who is one with Me and My Holy Spirit and there is no other way to heaven except through Jesus.

Wisdom 12:13 For neither is there any God besides.

23/11/97 Father
In the Eucharist you will find all you need to come closer to Me.
In the Eucharist you will find all you need to live your life in My love.

In the Eucharist you will find My Son waiting to answer your needs in bringing you closer to Me so that you can be complete in My love in My Son, Jesus.

Psalms 63:12 Rejoice in God.

23/11/97 Jesus
My love is there in My body and blood for all who seek it and for all who need it.
My love is there in the Eucharist offered to all but accepted by few.
My love is there in the Sacrament that says here I am unite with Me.
The Eucharist, the Sacrament that brings you to unite in My eternal body and blood as a sign of My love for you.

John 5:40 Come to me to have life.

24/11/97 Jesus
The gift I give to you in the Eucharist is beyond your comprehension, for if you were to understand the complete truth of My body and blood that you receive to unite you with Me, you would be so ecstatic you could not live.

Zechariah 2:17 In the presence of the Lord.

03/12/97 Jesus
Be one with Me in love,
Be one with Me in hope,
Be one with Me in giving all in the Eucharist.

Sirach 44:22 The covenant.

05/12/97 Jesus
Open your heart in the Eucharist to Me and allow My Holy Spirit to fill you with His gifts and graces.

Psalms 119:80 Be wholehearted
2 Maccabees 4:35 As a result.

07/12/97 Jesus
My presence in the Eucharist is the mystery of divinity offering unity to man.

My presence in the Eucharist is the mystery of divinity becoming flesh and blood for the salvation of man.

My presence in the Eucharist is the mystery of divinity loving man in a way that shows mankind how much God cares for them.

A mystery impossible for mankind to truly understand, and a mystery that needs faith to know.

Ezekiel 37:28 Thus the nations shall know that it is I the Lord.

21/12/97 Jesus
The mystery of life resides in the Eucharist.

23/12/97 Jesus
In the tabernacle of every church that believes in My
Eucharistic presence, I reside.
In the tabernacle of every church that is bound to Me in
the truth of the Sacrament, I reside.
In the tabernacle of every church that believes in My
body and blood present in the bread and wine, I reside.

*Ephesians 5:32 This is a great mystery but I speak in
reference to Christ and the church.*
Jeremiah 41:5 The house of the Lord.

28/12/97 Jesus
Embrace My love in the Eucharist and be filled with joy
from heaven.

Revelations 4:1 An open door to heaven.

29/12/97 Father
In the Eucharist place your soul and then in your soul find peace.

1 John 3:24 From the spirit that he gave us.

30/12/97 Jesus
In the Eucharist a priest should absorb himself totally so that through the Eucharist he can lead others to Me.

Job 41:9 So joined one to another that they hold fast and cannot be parted.

30/12/97 Jesus
The mercy poured out from My wounds on the cross is there for all people and that mercy can be found in each Eucharist.

Luke 1:50 His mercy is from age to age.

04/01/98 Father
Focusing on the Eucharist brings clarity to your work.
Focusing on the Eucharist keeps Jesus in your life.
Focusing on the Eucharist reminds you of the love Jesus has for you.

Jeremiah 31:35 Whose name is the Lord of hosts.
Psalms 24:5 Their saving God.

08/01/98 Jesus
In a priest's hands is the gift of consecration of the host.
No other can do it, no other is gifted in this way.
Respect priests and respect the gift I give to you in the priests.

Sirach 24:21 He who serves me.

14/01/98 Jesus
From the Eucharist find every thing you need in life for
I am the Eucharist and I will fill all your needs; just
believe.

Psalms 51:14 Sustain in me.

14/01/98 Jesus
The truth is I am the bread of life and the truth is found
in the Eucharist.

Malachi 2:6 True doctrine.

14/01/98 Jesus
In union with Me all is possible, find that union in the
Eucharist.

Sirach 24:18 Come to me all you that yearn for me.

14/01/98 Jesus
The Last Supper, the first communion.

Songs 1:12 The king's banquet.

19/01/98 Jesus
In Me you will never want,
In Me you will never fear,
In Me you will never be lost,
Find Me in the Eucharist.

30/03/98 Mother
Put on the heart of love,
Put on the spirit of grace,
Put on the soul of the Saviour,
In the Eucharist and in all the Sacraments God offers to
you.

Psalms 67:7 God, our God blesses us.

01/04/98 St Joachim
In the bread of life find true peace, true love and true
life when you find Jesus Christ.

Psalms 68:6 God whose abode is holy.

15/04/98 Jesus
In My body,
In My blood,
In My sacrament
Find all your needs fulfilled and all your longings for
love answered.

1 Samuel 26:20 From the presence of the Lord.

16/04/98 Jesus
In the Sacrament of love you will find Me waiting in the
Sacrament that is the Eucharist.

*John 21:13 Jesus came over and took the bread and
gave it to them.*

03/05/98 Jesus
The joy of uniting in My love is there for everyone in every Eucharist if only they believe.

Sirach 24:18 Come to me all you that yearn for me and be filled with my fruits.

13/05/98 Jesus
In My body you will find peace,
In My blood you will find security,
In the Eucharist you will find Me.

Proverbs 2:7 The shield for those who walk honestly.

22/05/98 Jesus
When you enjoy the Sacrament of the Eucharist you begin to celebrate and unite in My love.

25/05/98 Jesus
When you celebrate My love in the Eucharist you celebrate the greatest gift I give to mankind today...Myself.

Sirach 2:18 The mercy that he shows.

03/06/98 Jesus
Within the Eucharistic bread and wine awaits love for all time.
Within the Eucharistic celebration is forgiveness for every nation.
Within the Eucharistic sacrifice is the gift of My forgiving love, which is offered to all nations who only need to accept it was for them I paid the price.

2 Chronicles 17:10 All the kingdoms
Nahum 1:5 The world and all who dwell in it.

07/06/98 Jesus
The light of life,
The light of love,
The light of God,
All found in the Eucharist,
All found in Me and all found in the Trinity.

Sirach 30:1 He who loves.

13/06/98 Jesus
In each celebration of the Holy Mass I wait in love for
My children to come to Me and accept the wonderful
gift of love I offer to them.

Jeremiah 15:20 For I am with you.

20/06/98 Jesus
Being one with Me is offered to all in the Eucharist.
Being united with Me is offered in each Mass.
Being joined to Me for eternity is offered to each person
and in each Mass they can experience a little of this.

Psalms 63:5 I will bless you.

21/06/98 Jesus
A strong heart is needed to do My work for it is hard
work and it is work that places many demands on those
who do it. To find the strength they need to carry on all
My servants should come to Me and place themselves
deep into My heart where there is never-ending
strength.

My heart is found in the Eucharist and so to serve Me and to have the strength to do so, all who do My work must try to live a Eucharistic life, for this is where all their needs are answered.

Esther 7:2 Whatever you ask.
Psalms 102:21 To release those doomed to die.

22/6/98 Jesus
Feel My presence within you,
Feel My love within you,
Feel Me within you,
When you receive Me in Communion.

1 Corinthians 16:2 When I come.

22/06/98 Jesus
My love, My heart, My self,
All in the Eucharist, for that is where I am.

Matthew 26:26 This is my body
Matthew 26:28 This is my blood.

28/06/98 Jesus
In every Eucharist I wait to fill hearts and souls with My love.
In every Eucharist I offer each person unity with Me.
In every Eucharist I want every person to find peace as they unite in heart and soul with Me.

Daniel 9:23 Because you are beloved.

24/07/98 Jesus
A Eucharistic life is a Catholic life, for without the Eucharist in your life how can you truly be called a Catholic.

Psalms 63:6 My soul shall savour the rich banquet.

27/07/98 Jesus
Each Eucharist, a gift of My forgiving love to mankind.
Each Eucharist, a gift of My graces to mankind.
Each Eucharist, a gift of Myself to mankind.

Isaiah 66:14 When you see this your heart shall rejoice.

28/07/98 Jesus
In the Eucharist find peace,
In the Eucharist find safety,
In the Eucharist find Me and be at peace, safe in My love.

Isaiah 54:10 My love shall never leave you nor my covenant of peace be shaken.

29/07/98 Jesus
It is through meditating on the Eucharist that much will be revealed.

John 19:37 They will look upon him.

01/08/98 Jesus
The love that is to be found in the Eucharist is beyond mankind's comprehension. Even so, it is there for each person.

Job 33:7 My presence
Psalms 31:22 Wondrous love.

02/08/98 Jesus
United with Me in the Eucharist all people can find happiness, it is only they who can stop this.

Sirach 30:20 So it is with the afflicted man who groans at the good things his eyes behold.

12/08/98 Jesus
In the Eucharist all people are offered unity with Me and to have their entire beings filled with Me.
It is an offer that is there for all people.
How sad it is that many have not been told of this offer.

Acts 28:26 Go to this people.

12/08/98 Jesus
In the bread and wine is union with the divine.
In the bread and wine is salvation for all time.
In the bread and wine is the gift of love that is Mine.

2 Corinthians 9:11 You are being enriched in every way.

20/08/98 Father
Love resides in every Eucharist,
Love exists in every Eucharist,
Love is every Eucharist.

Isaiah 30:20 The Lord will give you the bread you need.

26/08/98 Jesus
In the Eucharist I am present and when you receive Me
in Communion then in you I am present.

*John 15:11 So that my joy might be in you and your joy
might be complete.*

01/09/98 Jesus
The Eucharist…My great gift of love for the world.
The Eucharist…My great gift of hope for the world.
The Eucharist…My great gift of Myself for the world.

*Titus 2:13-14 The blessed hope, the appearance of the
glory of the great God and of our saviour Jesus Christ
who gave himself.*

02/09/98 Jesus
The mystery of the Eucharist is beyond the
understanding of man but it becomes obvious in the
faith of love.

Proverbs 1:6 That he may comprehend.

08/09/98 Jesus
When you receive My body and blood think of My love
filling you, engulfing you and making you one with Me.
As you do this you will open your very soul to Me and
you will accept the greatest gift of all into your life.

Psalms 52:10 God's faithful love.

09/09/98 Jesus
The joy of the Eucharist is the joy of heaven touching
your soul.

Acts 10:33 The presence of God.

22/09/98 Jesus
The Eucharist brings life to souls,
The Eucharist bring souls to life...The Eucharist is life
itself.

Romans 9:26 The living God.

13/10/98 Jesus
Through the Eucharist find the cross and find the
strength to love it.

Psalms 34:6 Look to God.
*Luke 1:68 For he has visited and brought redemption to
his people.*

29/10/98 Father
With love in the centre of your heart, your heart
becomes one in Jesus for He is love and His love is
found in the Eucharist, so fill your heart there.

John 5:42 The love of God.

10/11/98 Jesus
To see a priest celebrating Mass is to see an image of
Me before you.

Romans 15:16 Performing the priestly service.

22/11/98 Jesus
United in the Eucharist are all who have partaken in My
body and blood.
United in the Eucharist are all those who have accepted
this most sacred of all gifts within.
United in the Eucharist, united in Me.
Psalms 51:8 In my inmost being.

24/11/98 Jesus
A Eucharistic life is one of love.
A Eucharistic life is one full of blessings.
A Eucharistic life is one all are called to.

Proverbs 8:4 To you O men I call.

26/11/98 Holy Spirit
When you hunger for My love you will find your desire fulfilled in the Eucharist, where when you receive Jesus, you will find I come with Him also.

2 Timothy 1:6 To stir into flame the gift of God you have.

02/12/98 Jesus
To be filled with My love come to the Eucharist for that is where I am and that is where you will find My love.

Luke 1:53 The hungry he has filled
Isaiah 66:11 With delight.

03/12/98 Jesus
The Eucharist truly is the doorway to heaven for I am the Eucharist.

Luke 2:13 The heavenly host.

08/12/98 Jesus
Life begins and ends in the Eucharist for I am the Eucharist and I am the beginning and the end.

Jeremiah 17:13 The source of living waters.

08/12/98 Jesus
The gift of the Eucharist is the greatest gift of all and the greatest prayer of all and to offer it for My Mother today brings her immense joy.

Songs 6:12 The blessed one of my kinswomen.

09/12/98 Jesus
Celebrate our love in the Eucharist, our love becoming one in Me.

1 Maccabees 14:11 Filled with happiness.

15/12/98 Jesus
Sanctity is found in Me,
Holiness is found in Me,
Eternal love is found in Me
And I am found in the Eucharist.

Luke 1:53 Filled with good things.

19/12/98 Jesus
In union with Me your soul shines brightly.
In union with Me your soul grows in grace.
In union with Me you soul is filled with eternal love.
In the Eucharist.

Daniel 12:3 Shine brightly
Psalms 119:149 In your love O Lord.

24/12/98 St Paul
In every Eucharist you should see the birth, death and resurrection of our Lord, for in every Eucharist is the life of Christ.

2 Timothy 2:11 Live with him.

27/12/98 Jesus
The joy of My love is found in the Eucharist for that is where I am and that is the truth.

Matthew 22:16 The truth.

29/12/98 Jesus
When you spend time before Me in adoration you will find peace and grace filling you.

Hosea 6:2 In his presence.

01/01/99 Jesus
To begin the year by celebrating the Eucharist is the best celebration to have as a welcome to the year ahead.

02/01/99 Father
The church must be Eucharistic.
The people must live a Eucharistic life.
The world will then change and all because of the Eucharist.

Psalms 95:7 For this is our God.

52.

05/01/99 Jesus
In each Eucharist resides My love waiting to embrace and fill each person who looks for Me.
In each Eucharist the door to My heart opens to each person inviting them to unite in My love.
In each Eucharist an abundance of My love is there to heal, to comfort and to bring peace to those who need it.
All this is there in the Eucharist, for in the Eucharist I am.

Luke 22:19 This is my body.

05/01/99 Jesus
In every Eucharist is the mystery of My divine love and to share in this mystery it is important to ask the Holy Spirit to show you how. Then follow wherever My spirit leads you for He will surely lead you deeper into My heart and deeper into the mystery of My love.

Titus 3:5 By the holy spirit.

06/01/99 Jesus
When you receive My body and blood you become one with Me, and in Me, united with everyone else who ever has or ever will receive Me.

1 Thessalonians 4:17 Shall always be with the lord.

09/01/99 Jesus
If you are looking for peace in your life, come to Me
If you are looking for hope in your life, come to Me
If you are looking for love in your life, come to Me.
Come to Me in the Eucharist for I am there waiting to fill you with peace, to bring you hope and to give you My love; just come to Me.

Isaiah 60:5 Your heart shall throb and overflow.

15/01/99 Jesus
The greatest prayer,
The greatest gift,
The greatest sight of God's love...The Eucharist.

Acts 10:33 All here in the presence of God.

16/01/99 Jesus
The joy of the Eucharist,
The love of the Eucharist,
The gift of the Eucharist,
Is all of Me for you and for all.

1 Corinthians 15:28 So that God may be all in all.

23/01/99 Jesus
With My body and blood filling your soul every time you receive Me within, your soul becomes more and more like Me.

Romans 8:29 Conformed to the image of his Son.

54.

27/01/99 Jesus
Every time a priest celebrates the Eucharist he becomes one in Me and with all the priests who ever have and ever will partake of this celebration.

Philippians 2:12 You have always been.

28/01/99 St Thomas Aquinas
To love the Eucharist is to love God.

Romans 15:29 In the fullness of Christ's blessing.

30/01/99 Father
To long for the Eucharist is a grace that will grow if you allow it by thinking on what Jesus gives to you in each one. He gives you Himself.

1 Timothy 4:4 When received with thanksgiving.

03/02/99 Jesus
The Eucharist is filled with love for all.
The Eucharist is an offering of My love for all.
The Eucharist is a waiting in love for all.

06/02/99 Jesus
To receive My body and blood is a gift I offer to all so that they can unite in eternity with Me and experience My divine love in their lives.

Galatians 3:28 All one in Christ.

08/02/99 Jesus

In the presence of My body and blood you are filled with graces and strengthened with My love. So the more time you spend with Me the stronger you will be.

Sirach 40:26 Seek no other support.

11/02/99 Jesus

To encourage partaking of the Eucharist is to encourage partaking of My love.

2 Corinthians 7:13 For this reason we are encouraged.

56.

24/02/99 St Praetextus
Holy love,
Divine love,
Glorious love…
God!

Living love,
Sacred love,
Trinitarian love…
The Eucharist!

Pure love,
Perfect love,
Precious love…
Jesus!

Jesus, the pure love of God living in each Eucharist, waiting to bring each person to holiness as His divine love touches them and opens their hearts to the glorious love of the Sacred Trinity that is God.

Psalms 17:7 Your wonderful love.

02/03/99 Jesus
A joy-filled celebration…The Eucharist.
A love-filled celebration…The Eucharist.
A God-filled celebration…The Eucharist.
I am there waiting to fill all with My joy and with My love in the Eucharist.

Ecclesiastes 5:19 The joy of his heart.

09/03/99 Jesus
The power of the Eucharist is beyond mankind's understanding but it should not be beyond their belief.

Ephesians 2:8 It is the gift of God.

09/03/99 Jesus
When your heart aches for My love, satisfy that desire in the Eucharist.

Ezekiel 2:8 Eat what I shall give you
Psalms 146:7 Food to the hungry.

16/03/99 Father
When you offer the Eucharist you offer the greatest and most powerful prayer of all for you offer the life, death, and resurrection of My Son Jesus.

Luke 10:19 Behold I have given you the power.

17/03/99 Jesus
In the Eucharist you will find yourself part of Me and part of My eternal life.

John 12:26 Where I am, there also will my servant be.

20/03/99 Jesus
At the centre of your faith must be the Eucharist.

29/03/99 Jesus
To offer the Eucharist for peace is the most powerful peace offering you can make, for the Eucharist is filled with My peace.

1 Maccabees 14:11 He brought peace to the land.

09/04/99 Jesus
In the Eucharist I am and you must be also.

12/04/99 St Theresa of Avilla
Your heart will be strengthened as you unite with the heart of Jesus in the Eucharist.

17/04/99 Jesus
In the Eucharist if you die to self you can come to life in Me.

Wisdom 18:18 Revealing the reason for his dying
2 Maccabees 14:46 The Lord of life.

19/04/99 Jesus
There is all you need in the Eucharist for I am there waiting to give you more than you could ever desire.

Isaiah 40:11 He feeds his flock.

09/05/99 Jesus
In each Eucharist I am there for you and all I ask is that you are there for Me and that you place yourself within Me.

Psalms 109:22 Within me.

13/05/99 Father
With the Eucharist as your focus in life, you focus on God and are opened to receive many graces.

13/05/99 Jesus
With the Eucharist in your life you truly begin to live. With the Eucharist in your heart you truly begin to love. With the Eucharist in your soul you truly begin to grow spiritually.

The Eucharist should be the love of your life if you want to nourish your soul and you seek to grow in My divine love.

Luke 2:13 The heavenly host.

14/05/99 Jesus
In every Eucharist you can open your heart to Me in love but the choice is yours to do so.

15/05/99 Jesus
With your heart residing in the Eucharist you become one in divinity but not divine.

With your heart residing in the Eucharist your humanity becomes graced in holiness.

With your heart residing in the Eucharist you come to life in the spirit as My holiness fills your very soul with My divinity.

Sirach 3:8 That his blessing may come upon you.

03/06/99 St Benedict
The cross can be seen in every Eucharist.

04/06/99 Jesus
In the bread of life,
In the wine of forgiveness,

In the body of your saviour,
In the blood of sacrifice,

In the Eucharist all came to be, for I am the Eucharist
from the beginning and forever.

04/06/99 Jesus
What you see before you in each Eucharist is eternal,
for I am the Eucharist.

Psalms 100:5 The Lord, whose love endures forever.

05/06/99 Jesus
In Me you will succeed, in self you will fail, so always
keep in Me through the Eucharist.

06/06/99 Father
In the body and blood of My Son Jesus find security,
peace and love.
In the body and blood of My Son Jesus find your true
home.
In the body and blood of My Son Jesus find eternity.

10/06/99 Father

It is important to be at peace within your heart, for without peace in your heart your life will be one of uncertainty.

To find the peace you need, turn to My Son Jesus in the Eucharist and be filled with the only peace that is true peace.

18/06/99 Jesus

The richness of life that many seek can be found through Me.

The richness of spirit that many seek can be found in Me.

The richness of grace that many seek can be found in union with Me...All found in the Eucharist.

18/06/99 Jesus

Hearts are hungry for My love.

Souls are empty without My love.

Spirits are in need of My love.

In every Eucharist I open My heart to touch souls and fill them with My spirit of love so that the hungry do not leave empty, as I answer all their needs.

07/07/99 Jesus

In the Eucharist find My strength there for you.

In the Eucharist find My love waiting to fill you.

In the Eucharist find Me waiting to unite you in My love and fill you with all the strength you need in this life.

10/07/99 Jesus

The bread, My body.

The wine, My blood.

The Eucharist, My gift to mankind.

15/07/99 Jesus
In each Eucharist eternity exists and yet within eternity the Eucharist is.
A divine mystery of time that the human mind will never unravel but it is one many will come to know when they come to My eternal love in heaven.

1 Corinthians 2:7 mysterious, hidden

17/07/99 Jesus
Within each Eucharist find the mystery of My life, My death, and My resurrection. It is there if you look.

Matthew 23:18 The gift on the altar.

26/07/99 Jesus
With the Eucharist filling your life, it becomes a life of love.

Proverbs 7:18 Fill of love.

28/07/99 Jesus
My precious blood mingles with yours when you receive My blood in the Eucharist.
My divine body fills yours when you receive My body in the Eucharist.
My sacred soul lifts yours in union with Mine when you become one in My body and blood in the Eucharist.

Matthew 23:30 Joined
Philippians 4:10 In the Lord.

31/07/99 Jesus
In the Eucharist you will find life itself.
In the Eucharist you will find the strength you need to live.
In the Eucharist you will find the joy of true life, for you will find Me.

John 6:57 Who feeds on me will have life because of me.

22/08/99 Jesus
In each Eucharist is the way to heaven.
In each Eucharist is the strength needed to reach heaven.
In each Eucharist is the door to heaven.

I am the Eucharist and in Me you will find the strength to walk the way to heaven, where I will be waiting with the door open wide.

Mark 10:24 To enter the kingdom of God.

22/08/99 Jesus
True soul food is found in the Sacrament of the Eucharist for it is the food of God Himself.

Zepheniah 2:10 The Lord of hosts.

06/09/99 Jesus
You have your strength in Me every time you come and receive Me in the Eucharist.

64.

08/09/99 Jesus
My body,
My blood,
My soul,
My divinity…
There in the Eucharist to bring you to sanctity.

21/09/99 Jesus
The Eucharist is an offering of My love to you and when you receive My love in thanks and in love, then united in Me, whatever you offer in love, becomes a powerful prayer.

Jeremiah 3:23 In the Lord
Psalms 96:6 Power
Romans 8:28 For those who love God.

23/09/99 Jesus
Within My body, blood, soul and divinity you can become the spirit of love that you were created to be and in that spirit bring Me to all you meet.

You can do this by coming to Me in every Eucharist and saying from your heart, 'I believe, Lord use me.' Then in union with Me you can open your heart to all you meet and let My love and yours embrace them.

John 11:25 Whoever believes in me
Psalms 89:25 Love will be with him.

26/09/99 Jesus
The majesty,
The grace,
The power,
The love,
In each priest celebrating the Eucharist is beyond the comprehension of mankind but is known in heaven and is feared in hell.

Luke 3:2 The high priesthood.

30/09/99 Jesus
In the Eucharist is My life if you look and see.

Romans 9:26 The living God.

03/10/99 Jesus
Through the Eucharist people can find holiness.
Through the Eucharist people can find their true selves.
Through the Eucharist people can find that it is in Me people will find themselves made holy.
When people totally believe, accept and live in this divine mystery, is when people will become holy.

Deuteronomy 4:26 Live in it.

10/10/99 Jesus
Eucharistic joy,
Eucharistic happiness,
Eucharistic love is there for all people who believe and seek Me in every Mass.

66.

17/10/99 Jesus
In every Eucharist your soul receives the food of eternal joy.

Psalms 27:13 Enjoy the Lord's goodness.

18/10/99 Jesus
My body and blood will bring you to sanctity.
My body and blood will bring you to unite with divinity.
My body and blood will bring you to heaven if you believe and live in Me.

28/10/99 Jesus
As you come to Me in the Eucharist, you come to life.

16/11/99 Father
The power that drives your heart is My love and so the more you receive My Son Jesus in the Eucharist, the more powerful your heart will be.

Isaiah 66:14 The Lord's power.

23/11/99 Jesus
Your heart is one in Mine in the Eucharist and then in the Eucharist your heart can become as Mine for others.

02/12/99 Jesus
The Eucharist can make your life complete when you believe and accept My presence into your life.

05/12/99 Jesus
As you look into the Eucharist, look with eyes of love and you will find what you desire.

Isaiah 17:7 His eyes turned towards the holy one of Israel.

10/12/99 Jesus
In the Eucharist you can grow in holiness and grow in grace.

10/12/99 Jesus
The power of heaven resides in the Eucharist and therefore resides in those who receive Me in the Eucharist.

John 11:26 Everyone who lives and believes in me.

12/12/99 Jesus
The true food for the soul is found in the Eucharist and it is by this soul food that a person can grow in grace and holiness.

John 6:51 The living bread that came down from heaven.

16/12/99 Jesus
Taken within, My body and blood transforms your soul to become one in Me.

1 Corinthians 10:15 The cup of blessing that we bless, is it not a participation in the blood of Christ. The bread that we break is it not a participation in the body of Christ.

17/12/99 St Olympias
The mystery of God,
The majesty of God,
The mercy of God,
Can all be found in the Eucharist.

1 Timothy 1:2 Grace, mercy and peace from God.

17/12/99 Jesus
When you receive Me within the Eucharist with love, it is no wonder you smile, for inside of you your soul is dancing with joy.

Philippians 2:18 Your joy with me.

19/12/99 Jesus
To celebrate the Eucharist with joy in your heart is a sign of your true love of Me.

22/12/99 Father
The food that sustains for eternity is the Eucharist.

23/12/99 Father
If you wash yourself in the blood and water of My Son Jesus at every Eucharist then your very being reflects His divine mercy and wherever you go you bring His mercy with you.

Genesis 49:11 In wine he washes his garments, his robe in the blood of grapes.

26/12/99 Jesus
Every day is a feast day when you come to My banquet in the Eucharist.

31/12/99 Jesus
Washed in the Eucharist,
Washed in My blood,
Washed in My love.

1 Peter 1:19 With the precious blood of Christ.

09/01/00 Jesus
In the Eucharist you come to true life.

Hosea 6:2 To live in his presence.

10/01/00 Jesus
The Eucharist is offered to all people and those who know of My treasure within the Eucharist should tell all people what awaits them there.

2 Corinthians 10:10 His bodily presence.

11/01/00 Jesus
My power resides in the Eucharist and when you reside in the Eucharist so My power resides in you.

Isaiah 40:10 Here comes with power the Lord God.
Romans 1:16 It is the power of the God.

16/01/00 Holy Spirit
For your spirit to grow to its full potential on earth the Eucharist is essential.

Romans 6:5 Grown into union with him.

17/01/00 Jesus
My church stands upon the Eucharist and any church that does not is not truly My church and does not stand on Me but stands in a protesting pride.

1 Corinthians 11:22 You show contempt for the church of God.

06/02/00 Padre Pio
Blessed are they who receive Our Divine Lord in love in the Eucharist.

06/02/00 Padre Pio
In the Eucharistic light of Christ a person can illuminate the world.

06/02/00 Padre Pio
When you think in love about the Eucharist you open your very soul to many graces, graces which will bring you to eternal joy.

27/02/00 Father
In every Eucharist is the doorway to eternal glory.

28/02/00 Jesus
Without My true presence in the Eucharist the Holy Mass is empty and all those who celebrate the Eucharist, whatever the denomination, should remember this and come to live in the true Eucharistic faith.

02/03/00 Jesus
Whether it is a Eucharistic union or a spiritual union, due to you being unable to get to Mass, it is a union with Me that lifts your soul into My divinity.

05/03/00 Father
The divine love of My Son Jesus is waiting in every Eucharist to fill hearts with peace, with joy, with contentment and with His divine truth.

09/03/00 Father
The love of the Eucharist should be in the heart of every Catholic.

11/03/00 Father
To reflect on My love in your life, reflect upon the Eucharist.

18/03/00 Jesus
To take My love into your soul come to the Eucharist and receive Me in love.

Sirach 8:19 Open your heart.

72.

28/03/00 Father
The Eucharist today, like every day, will fill you with
divine joy if you let it.

01/04/00 Jesus
To be one in Me is possible in every Eucharist.

John 14:15 If you love me.

04/04/00 Jesus
Our hearts unite in every Eucharist and so the more you
come to the Eucharist the more you are united with Me.

14/04/00 Father
Find your strength in the Eucharist,
Find your gifts in the Eucharist,
Find yourself in the Eucharist and you will be gifted by
My Son Jesus with the strength you need.

*Psalms 46:12 The Lord of hosts is with us; our
stronghold is the God of Jacob.*

17/04/00 Jesus
My heart is one with the Father's heart and Our Spirit's
heart is one in Our one heart. The heart that all can be
one in through the Eucharistic offer I make in every
Mass.

Acts 10:36 Through Jesus Christ, who is Lord of all.

18/04/00 Jesus
In the Eucharist I am and so can you be by giving yourself to Me in each one.

Luke 5:18 In his presence.

24/04/00 Jesus
A joyful celebration of My love,
A sorrowful celebration of My love,
A divine mystery of My love...
The Eucharist.

12/05/00 Jesus
Now you are filled with Me in the Eucharist, go and help others to be filled with Me also.

23/05/00 Jesus
To the world I give Myself each day in every Eucharist.

Hosea 6:2 His presence.

31/05/00 Jesus
Each Eucharist is full of joy; joy for everyone who seeks and accepts it in humble love of Me.

15/06/00 Father
The heart of a person grows to be a beautiful flower of love when it is fed the body and blood of My Son Jesus in the Eucharist and when Jesus, My Son is accepted completely into the person's heart.

74.

16/06/00 Jesus
Many seek a renewal of faith.
Many seek a renewal of life.
Many seek a renewal of love.
It is in the Eucharist all people can be renewed and find
their faith comes alive in My love.

25/06/00 Father
In the Eucharist you will find all the answers you need
to live a fulfilling life.

25/06/00 Father
In the Mass your heart grows and so if you go
frequently to Mass your heart grows more and more.

25/06/00 Jesus
Trust in My body,
Believe in My blood,
And find your prayers answered.

05/07/00 Jesus
In a priest celebrating the Eucharist see My gift of grace
to the world.

09/07/00 Father
The light of My Son Jesus fills the souls of all those
who receive Him in love in the Eucharist. While only
darkness fills the souls of many of those who do not.

10/07/00 Father
Make the Eucharist the centre of your day then the day
becomes one centered in love.

10/07/00 Jesus
When you rest in My heart you are renewed in My love.
When you hide in My heart you are protected from harm.
When you remain in My heart you are assured heaven will be yours.
My heart, found in every Eucharist.

Isaiah 58:11 He will renew your strength and you shall be like a watered garden, like a spring whose water never fails.

10/07/00 Jesus
My love and your love become one in the Eucharist.

15/07/00 Father
When you feel empty within turn to My Son Jesus in the Eucharist and be filled with all you need in Him.

19/07/00 Jesus
Each Eucharist you partake of lifts you closer to heaven and brings you nearer to Me.

19/07/00 Jesus
The power in the Eucharist fills your heart and soul each time you receive My body and My blood. The power in which you can rely upon to overcome any evil you may face.

Ephesians 3:16 Strengthened with power.

22/07/00 Jesus
Every Eucharist is a vision of love to behold.

76.

22/07/00 Jesus
Your soul is filled with Me in every communion of love
in the Eucharist.

25/07/00 Jesus
The lifting of your spirit that you feel in every Eucharist
is your soul becoming one in Mine.

Ephesians 5:31 The two shall become one.

17/08/00 Jesus
By opening your heart in love of Me in the Eucharist,
you become filled with My love and with the graces and
gifts that come with it.

18/08/00 Mother
Every Eucharist celebrated on earth is celebrated in
heaven too.

21/08/00 Jesus
In the moments you experience, when you receive My
body and blood, is the mystery of My love feeding your
soul.

Acts 2:28 You fill me with joy in your presence.

25/08/00 Jesus
The life of a follower of Mine must be Eucharistic if he
truly wants to live in Me.

Romans 8:1 Life in Christ Jesus.

26/08/00 Jesus
The bread of the Eucharist becomes perfect at the consecration when it becomes the bread of life. The wine of Communion becomes perfect at the consecration when it becomes the wine of salvation.

The bread and the wine of the Eucharist become perfect at the consecration when they become My body and My blood, then in Communion each person can be filled with that perfection which is My perfect love.

Matthew 5:48 Is perfect
Philippians 2:1 In love
James 1:17 Perfect gift is from above.

26/08/00 Jesus
To celebrate properly the Eucharist is only possible with love in your heart and the humility to understand that it is by the power of My Holy Spirit that you are able to do so.

Acts 8:15 The holy spirit.

27/08/00 Jesus
The Eucharist can bring people to true life if they truly believe in My presence in the Eucharist and in My presence in them when they receive Me in Communion.

01/09/00 Jesus
United in My love,
One in My body,
Joined in My blood,
As you embrace Me in the Eucharist this is what you become.

10/09/00 Jesus
To be truly Eucharistic a person must be loving.

09/10/00 St Denis
Live in the Eucharist for without it, is there truly life?

13/10/00 Father
The priestly life led by those who have lived their promise to Me, is a life that fills eternity with joy.

Each Eucharist a priest celebrates is eternal and in that celebration of love the priest himself becomes part of that eternal moment where My Son's presence becomes real as the bread and wine is turned into His Holy body and blood.

The priest in this moment enters into the eternal moment of love, which in turn brings to fulfillment his priestly life as the priest accepts and believes in the true presence of My Son Jesus.

15/10/00 Jesus
In My light you illuminate all around you.
Stay in My light by staying in the Eucharist.

16/10/00 Jesus
It is with joy I wait for you to come to Me in every Eucharist.

22/10/00 Jesus
Eucharistic love I give to you. Now take My love to others.

24/10/00 Jesus
In the Eucharist people are united in My love and if they will remain Eucharistic people will remain united in Me.

03/11/00 Jesus
It is a great joy to me when people come to receive Me in the Eucharist because they love Me and want to be closer to Me.

04/11/00 Jesus
As you live a Eucharistic life, My grace in you grows to reach out from your very soul and to touch other souls you come in contact with and to give them the desire to live in Me too.

12/11/00 Jesus
To celebrate the Eucharist properly, a person must be seeking Me within it.

14/11/00 Jesus
As you grow in My Eucharistic love, you grow in grace and in faith.

Numbers 19:3 In his presence.

19/11/00 Jesus
Your soul magnifies My love every time you receive
Me in the Eucharist and then take Me to others.

Colossians 2:2 Together in love.

10/12/00 Father
Just as worldly food is essential for your body, so is
heavenly food essential for your soul. My Son Jesus is
the bread of heaven all should eat of if they want to
nourish their soul in grace.

*Psalms 107:9 For he satisfied the thirsty, filled the
hungry with good things.*

06/01/01 Jesus
The Holy Spirit is there through the Eucharist waiting to
help people open their hearts and souls to Me.

23/01/01 Jesus
Through the Eucharist you will find holiness.
Through the Eucharist you can grow in holiness.
Through the Eucharist you can become holy.
In the Eucharist you will find Me and if you can accept
this and live in Me, you will find through Me you grow
and grow in holiness.

31/01/01 Jesus
As you come to Me in the Eucharist, come in expectant
love and find your expectation fulfilled.

04/02/01 Jesus
In every Eucharist I am with you and when you receive
Me you are with Me.

1 John 2:5 In union with him.

08/02/01 Jesus
Each moment you spend in adoration of Me and with
Me is a grace-filled moment.

09/02/01 Jesus
At every meal remember My Last Supper and
remember the true food of life I offer for mankind in
every Eucharist.

12/02/01 Jesus
The Eucharist is filled with joy and so can be those who
participate in it when they give themselves totally to Me
in the Eucharist.

06/03/01 Jesus
My happiness,
My joy,
My love,
All found in My body and blood which is the Eucharist.

Psalms 13:6 Joy in your
Job 31:23 God.

11/03/01 Father
In every Eucharist you can grow in My grace through
My Son Jesus and through Him be filled with the power
of My Holy Spirit when you open your heart in love to
receive the body and blood of My Divine Son within.

11/03/01 Jesus
As My blood washes over your soul and My body fills
it with My love, you become more like Me, and so does
everyone who accepts in love My Eucharistic gift to
them.

12/03/01 Jesus
Love grows in the Eucharist for in the Eucharist love
resides.

12/03/01 Jesus
It is the way to find true love - the Eucharist.

18/03/01 Jesus
Joyfully is how the Eucharist should be celebrated.
Respectfully is how people should partake of the
Eucharist.
Hopefully is how the Eucharist is to be lived.

Jeremiah 31:17 There is hope for your future.

21/03/01 Jesus
In every Eucharist I pour out My love to fill every heart
that will receive and welcome Me in love.

23/03/01 Jesus
My pure love,
My divine love,
My sacrificial love...
Found in the Eucharist.

My merciful love,
My forgiving love,
My cleansing love...
Found in Reconciliation.

My holy love,
My true love,
My perfect love...
Found in the Sacraments of My One Holy Catholic Church which contains My perfect truth for all to live by in My love.

24/03/01 Jesus
In your heart is My love,
In your soul is My love,
In your spirit is My love,
For you are filled with My love in every Eucharist you receive.

25/03/01 Jesus
In the Holy Mass you can find holiness filling your soul and changing your life for the better when you believe in and accept My presence within.

Romans 1:7 To be holy.

11/04/01 Jesus
In My presence you grow in My graceful love and are gifted with presents to share with others.

12/04/01 Father
Remember the Last Supper was the first Eucharistic banquet.

16/04/01 Father
Let the light of My Son Jesus' love fill your soul in every Eucharist by offering yourself completely to Him at each one.

19/04/01 Jesus
Your heart and My heart...One in the Eucharist.

01/05/01 Mother
Let the love of God be in your heart always, by receiving His love in frequent Eucharist.

04/06/01 Archangel St Raphael
With you at every Eucharist are the heavenly hordes of angels bowing in adoration to the Divine Lord Jesus.

Psalms 34:8 The angel of the Lord, who encamps with them.

24/06/01 Father
The living bread,
The wine of life,
The divine food, which brings all people to life when they eat in love of the bread and wine which is the body and blood of My Son Jesus in the Eucharist.

25/06/01 Jesus
In the love of the Eucharist your love of Me grows.

26/06/01 Jesus
In every Eucharist I open My heart and say, 'I love you.'

03/07/01 St Thomas
In every Eucharist your faith can grow and your doubts can disappear if you ask Our Lord Jesus for the grace that they may do so.

25/07/01 Jesus
As you come to Me in the Eucharist seeking My love, so I pour out Myself to fill you with all you need to make your life complete.

02/08/01 Jesus
Beginning the day in My Eucharistic love is the best way to start the day.

13/08/01 Jesus
You can become holy in every Eucharist.

14/08/01 Jesus
Every day is a feast day when you come to Me in the Eucharist.

20/08/01 Jesus
In Me you can become one with God.
In Me you can become complete in God.
In Me you can become a complete person living with one heart, The heart of God.

20/08/01 Jesus
The most glorious event you will every experience in
your life on earth is becoming one with Me in the
Eucharist.

21/08/01 St Pius X
To be united with Christ is essential in living your faith,
for it is in the Eucharist you can find the grace you need
to do so.

1 Thessalonians 3:7 Your faith.

21/08/01 St Pius X
God gives Himself to mankind in every Eucharist and
mankind needs to thank God for this and give
themselves to Him in every Communion.

21/08/01 St Pius X
The greatest heresy today within the Church is that the
bread and wine of the Eucharist does not become the
body and blood of Christ Our Lord.
It is a heresy that needs to be confronted and defeated
by the faithful, so that all can come to believe in this
divine truth.

03/09/01 St Gregory the Great
In the words of Holy Scripture is a great gift from God
for mankind.
In the Holy Sacrifice of our Lord Jesus is the great
forgiveness of God for mankind.
In the Holy Eucharist is God for mankind.

19/09/01 Mother
When you pray you are opening your soul to God's love.

When you receive my Son Jesus in the Eucharist you are filling your soul with God's love.

When you work for God you are magnifying God's love within you, bringing His love into the lives of others so that they also may be filled with His love and come to know my Son Jesus in their lives too.

07/10/01 Jesus
In the Eucharist is all mankind needs to live a good life, for I am there and I am goodness itself.

26/10/01 Jesus
As you place yourself within the Eucharist you are absorbed into Me to become one in Me and I am absorbed into you to become one with you.

16/11/01 Mother
Let your heart be one with my Son Jesus in the Eucharist and then show Him in your heart to the world.

18/11/01 Jesus
In the Eucharist you can find completeness of life and fulfillment of spirit when you give yourself totally to Me and accept Me totally within.

02/12/01 Jesus
The food of the soul is My love found in the Eucharist, no where else.

13/12/01 Jesus
My real presence is in every Mass of every priest who is consecrated in the way of My Apostles and the teachings of My Holy Church.

25/12/01 Jesus
In the manger was placed the food of life for all people to come and eat of.

I am that food and I still offer the invitation to all people to come and eat of My divine body and blood so that they can find true life in Me.

An invitation made in every Eucharist for all people who will seek to live and love in Me.

06/01/02 Father
Find in the Eucharist true life and find the strength to live that life.

12/01/02 Jesus
In order to be like Me a person needs to be one with Me in the Eucharist.
It is here that My divinity will engulf and change a person who seeks to be like Me to be just that; an image of Me in the world.

12/01/02 Jesus
The highest spiritual level any person can achieve on earth is union with Me in the Eucharist.

13/01/02 Father
It is love that draws you to the Eucharist; My love in My Son Jesus.

16/01/02 Jesus
A grace-filled heart is one that lives the Eucharist.

16/01/02 Father
Those who receive My Son Jesus frequently in the Eucharist grow quickly in grace and if they share that grace I then grace them even more.

23/01/02 Father
To start your day in the Eucharist is the greatest way to start it.

24/01/02 Jesus
The happiness you experience in My Eucharistic love is a happiness to be shared and not kept to yourself.

30/01/02 Father
Let your heart go freely to My Son Jesus in every Eucharist and be filled with His joyful love.

04/02/02 Jesus
The holiest act you can do on earth is to receive Me in the Eucharist.

07/02/02 Jesus
In every Eucharist you can find your true self when you find and accept Me into your heart and soul.

08/02/02 Mother
The holiest place on earth is within every Eucharist.

Psalms 95:6 Bow down in worship; let us kneel before the Lord.

08/02/02 St John of Matha
To exercise your soul, pray.
To strengthen your soul, read Holy Scripture.
To fill your soul, receive the Lord Jesus in the Sacrament of the Eucharist.

09/02/02 Father
The loveliest person on earth is the one who has just received My Son Jesus in the Eucharist in love.

21/02/02 Father
Your soul is safe in the Eucharistic love of My Son Jesus.

22/02/02 Jesus
The greatest gift I can give to you is Myself in the Eucharist.

25/02/02 Jesus
It is by the power of My love that is found in the Eucharist that the world can be changed and brought to its senses.

25/02/02 Jesus
To be holy come and fill yourself with Me in the sacred gift of the Eucharist.

26/02/02 Jesus
When your heart unites in My Eucharistic heart then there is an explosion of love that reverberates throughout eternity.

28/02/02 Father
The desire to love Me grows each time you receive and accept My Son Jesus within you in the Eucharist.

05/03/02 Jesus
In every Eucharist you receive I am in you and you are in Me united in eternity.

08/03/02 Jesus
When you give yourself freely to Me in love in every Eucharist then your soul opens to be filled with the delight of My love, the power of My love, the joy of My love. Then it must be opened to share these with others when you leave the Eucharist and go with thanksgiving out to the world.

10/03/02 Jesus
The Eucharist is full of forgiveness and love, for it is full of Me. When you fill yourself with Me in the Eucharist you too must be then full of forgiveness and love.

10/03/02 Mother
Let my Son Jesus embrace you in the Eucharist. Let Him wrap Himself around you with His body and blood. Let Him fill you with His soul, His divinity. Let Him be one with you to change the core of your very being, to change it to be one of love, one of holiness, one of Him.

18/03/02 Jesus
To enter deep into My love is possible in the Eucharist.

27/03/02 Jesus
In every Eucharist your focus should be on Me from beginning to end.

28/03/04 (Holy Thursday) Jesus
Today it may have been The Last Supper but it was the first Eucharistic feast.

03/04/02 Jesus
With My body and blood within you, you can become more and more like Me; you can become loving, caring and kind.

15/04/02 Father
As you enter into the Sacrament of the Eucharist, open your soul to My Son by asking My Holy Spirit to help you in doing so and then be filled spiritually and physically with His love.

15/04/02 Jesus
Your soul is fed with the food of life that comes from heaven in every Eucharist. Eat freely of Me in every Eucharist and then live life freely in Me every day.

17/04/02 Jesus
Every moment spent in My presence is a moment I will remember when I present you to My Father.

19/04/02 Jesus
My beautiful love resides in every Eucharist and can reside in all who truly seek Me and receive Me in the Eucharist.

20/04/02 Jesus
In the Eucharist your soul is enriched, your spirit is strengthened and your body is refreshed in Me.

22/04/02 Father
In the heart of the Eucharist is the love-filled heart of My Son Jesus.

25/04/02 Jesus
Holiness fills you in every Eucharist.

27/04/02 Jesus
The greatest gift you can ever offer Me in your life is your love united in Mine in the Eucharist. A gift I long to receive from every person.

29/04/02 Jesus
In your heart is love of the Eucharist because in your soul you know I am the Eucharist.

03/05/02 St Philip, Apostle
The grace of God was seen in the Lord Jesus as He walked the earth.
The love of God was seen in the Lord Jesus as He came to earth.
The power of God was seen in the Lord Jesus as He was crucified, buried and rose again.
The same power by the grace of God, can be seen and experienced in every Eucharist where Jesus Our Lord reaches out to all people in love with His true presence, inviting each one to join in His glorious divinity so they can enjoy an intimate relationship with Him.

06/05/02 Mother
Daily prayer and daily Eucharist shows daily your love of God and helps you to grow in His love.

06/05/02 Jesus
The greatest gift I give to you is My love in the Eucharist.

10/05/02 Jesus
Joy-filled moments,
Love-filled moments,
Grace-filled moments,
The moments you spend in My presence bring Me great joy as you show your love for Me and allow your heart and soul to be opened and filled with My grace.

Psalms 16:11 Abounding joy in your presence.

18/05/02 Holy Spirit
In the whole world there is a vacuum of love that sin and evil has created. This vacuum needs to be filled with the Eucharistic love and power of Jesus, so that mankind can find true peace in the heart of God.

20/05/02 Father
The food you need to live eternity in bliss is My Son Jesus in the Eucharist.
Any other food will not sustain you.

01/06/02 Jesus
Your Eucharistic life is true life. Keep living it!

02/06/02 Jesus
My body,
My blood...
There for all My people who will believe.

02/06/02 Jesus
It is in My Eucharistic body and blood people can find a complete life on earth and then in heaven too.

02/06/02 Jesus
Anyone who does not believe in My true presence in the bread and wine of Communion does not believe in the words of Holy Scripture and therefore cannot truly believe in the fullness of My gift of life and faith to mankind.

02/06/02 Jesus
Those who reject and deny Me in the Eucharist deny themselves the greatest gift of all and reject the grace that comes with it.

22/06/02 Mother
Living the day in the Eucharist is the greatest way to live the day.

22/06/02 Jesus
Let My love grow in you by receiving My love in the Eucharist.

24/06/02 Jesus
Love of the Eucharist is truly love of God for I am God and I am the Eucharist.

24/06/02 Jesus
The greatest prayer of love you can offer is the Eucharist, for it is love; My divine love with your love united in Me.

05/07/02 Mother
Remember the power of the Eucharist and use it for good and for the betterment of mankind.

05/07/02 Jesus
As you live the Eucharist you truly begin to live.

Romans 8:2 Life in Christ Jesus.

07/07/02 Mother
To prepare for the Holy Eucharist ask the Holy Spirit to help you prepare.

09/07/02 Jesus
Miracles happen every day and if you want to see one come to the Eucharist and you will see the greatest of all.

11/07/02 Jesus
Rejoice in the Eucharist, for it is full of My joyful love and so should be those who receive Me in the Eucharist.

12/07/02 Jesus
In each Eucharist there is a manifestation of My spiritual and physical love for mankind.

18/07/02 Jesus
The Eucharist shows My love and if you look in love you will see it.

24/07/02 Jesus
Wherever you celebrate the Eucharist in love of Me the result is the same: an intimate union with Me.

01/08/02 Jesus
Hearts are opened in love.
Hearts are filled with love.
Hearts become love as they unite in My love in every Eucharist.

02/08/02 Jesus
Those who share in the Eucharist become one in Me and so it would be natural and correct to see Me in them.

03/08/02 Mother
As holy words come forth from the mouth of a priest during the Eucharist, eternity is filled with those words as they unite with all the holy words of every Eucharist ever celebrated.

03/08/02 Jesus
To be like Me you should fill yourself with Me in the Eucharist.

09/08/02 Jesus
The Eucharist is all powerful and the Rosary is all loving.
Together they can heal all.

09/08/02 Jesus
To begin the day in My Eucharistic love enables a person to live the whole day in the Eucharist.

09/08/02 Jesus
Every person who receives Me in love in the Eucharist is elevated to a higher level of their humanity as their spirituality is deepened in Me.

10/08/02 Jesus

As you grow in the love of the Eucharist you grow spiritually in Me.

11/08/02 Jesus

When the body is hungry it needs to be fed so that it will be healthy, strong and without hunger pangs. So it is with the soul, it too needs to be fed to remain healthy, strong and without hunger pangs.

To feed the body the food of earth is necessary.

To feed the soul the food of heaven is essential.

It is only this food that will satisfy completely spiritual hunger.

I am that food and I am found only in the Eucharist as the food of life for souls.

In the Eucharist there is enough of Me to feed, fill and satisfy every soul.

In the Eucharist I offer every soul the opportunity to feed on Me as they go on their way to heaven so that each one will have the strength to finish their journey.

13/08/02 Father

Each Eucharist you partake of is an opportunity to grow spiritually as you unite with the body, blood, soul and divinity of My Son Jesus. In the Eucharist His Spirit lifts yours to higher levels of grace and His body and blood, as it unites with yours, brings your physical human being to be changed by His divinity to be more like Him in His life, in His sufferings, in His death and in His resurrection.

The Eucharist…a life-changing gift which can change both your spiritual and physical life by bringing your entire being to holiness in and through My Son Jesus.

14/08/02 Jesus
To find Me in the Eucharist people must first lose themselves.

14/08/02 Jesus
In every Eucharist is the way to be more like Me as you accept Me within and unite with Me.

17/08/02 Jesus
Eucharistic love is true love as it is My love and love of Me.

19/08/02 Jesus
In the Eucharist man becomes one with God. Heaven and earth unite and what is finite becomes one with infinity.

19/08/02 Jesus
My Eucharistic heart waits to bring every heart to fullness of life and fullness of love in Me.

19/08/02 Jesus
In every Eucharist when you receive Me with an open and loving heart your soul is illuminated with My divine light.

19/08/02 Jesus
In the way you receive Me in the Eucharist you decide how you will experience Me.

If I am received in love, with humility, and with a deep desire to be one with Me, then people will experience My divine love uniting with their souls and bringing their entire being to peace within Me.

If I am received as a duty, with little love, with doubt, with disbelief or with self first, then people will experience little at all except maybe a misery of soul as they deny themselves the food souls thrive on and long for.

22/08/02 Father
Eucharistic love,
Eternal love,
Divine love…
Jesus My Son, My love.

25/08/02 Jesus
In Eucharistic adoration your very soul grows in grace
and matures in My love.

03/09/02 Jesus
The greatest gift I give to you is Myself in the Eucharist.

11/09/02 Jesus
The bread and wine,
Body and blood divine.

12/09/02 Jesus
In the Eucharist resides My love.
Live a Eucharistic life and live a life in My love so that one day you can reside with Me in heaven.

Psalms 22:27 May your hearts enjoy life forever.

17/09/02 Jesus
It is My love that will bring you to fullness of life; My love in the Eucharist.

22/09/02 Mother
It is in the Eucharist you will find my Son brings you to your true self; the self of love; His love.

27/09/02 Mother
Adoration of God is possible at all times but is greatest in His presence in the Eucharist.

27/09/02 Jesus
Regardless of the language, when the Eucharist is celebrated the words within it are Holy.

03/10/02 Father
In the Eucharist My Son Jesus unites heaven and earth.

05/10/02 Father
Your heart and My heart unite when you join with My Son Jesus in the Eucharist, for He is My heart of love.

05/10/02 Jesus
My Eucharistic power can heal any disease.

10/10/02 Jesus
When people find Me in the Eucharist they find true life and true love.

22/10/02 Jesus
The holiness of My love resides in the Eucharist and in all those who receive Me within in a communion of love.

23/10/02 Father
The greatest vision on earth is My Son Jesus in the Eucharist.

29/10/02 Mother
Eucharistic love is love of God.

07/11/02 Father
When the body is tired you rest and recover your strength.
When the soul is tired you too must rest so that the soul may be strengthened.
To rest the soul, a person only needs to come to My Son Jesus in the Eucharist and be at peace in Him in a union of love.

19/11/02 Jesus
In every Eucharist I reside and I ask all those who love Me to come and reside there too.

21/11/02 Mother
As you present yourself to the Lord each day in the Eucharist seeking His love, He fills you with His divine presence.

22/11/02 Father
With every Eucharist you partake of you come closer to Me in and through My Son Jesus.

10/12/02 Jesus
The Eucharist is where all the faithful should seek Me, for it is here they will find Me.

11/12/02 Father
To rest your soul, be at peace with My Son in adoration in His presence in the Blessed Sacrament.

11/12/02 Father
To nourish your soul,
To strengthen your spirit,
To grow in grace,
Eat of My Son Jesus in the Eucharist.

12/12/02 Jesus
Every time you receive Me in the Eucharist you receive all the strength you need to move mountains and to change the world for the better, for you receive My strength.

12/12/02 Jesus
Just as the body needs feeding so does the soul, and the food that feeds the soul is My heavenly body and blood found in the Eucharist.

17/12/02 Jesus

In the Eucharist people can, with the divine, unite and then, one with God, can reach the highest height.

In the Eucharist people can become one in Me and have their souls enriched by My divinity.

In the Eucharist people can find their hearts one in Mine and truly experience love divine.

18/12/02 Jesus

It is with great joy I unite in the Eucharist with those who love Me and it is with great joy they should receive Me.

21/12/02 Father

The more Eucharistic a person is the more like My Son Jesus they become.

22/12/02 St Paul

Any Christian who speaks against the true presence of Jesus Our Lord in the Eucharist or denies His presence in it are living in heresy.

Any Christian who denies or speaks against the authority and primacy given to Peter and to those who succeed him are living against the divine authority of God and place themselves in heresy.

Any Christian who denies or alters or speaks against the Word of God in Holy Scripture embraces heresy.

Sadly today many Christians do this as they follow the false and heretical teachings of those, who, in their zeal for reformation, deny Christ Our Lord and His Holy Words and promote their own understanding of God instead.

23/12/02 Jesus
In the Eucharist our hearts entwine the human and the divine.

23/12/02 Jesus
To climb the spiritual stairway to heaven a person needs the spiritual strength found in Me in every Eucharist.

30/12/02 Jesus
When you have joy because others receive Me in the Eucharist, it is a sign of your true love.

01/01/03 Mother
Place the Eucharist first in your life and you put God first in your life.

01/01/03 Jesus
With a heart strong in My Eucharistic love a person can achieve great good in this life and greatness in heaven in the next life.

08/01/03 Jesus
With love in your heart,
With love in your mind,
With love in your soul,
You have Me within you in the completeness of you and when you profess your true love of Me in the receiving of the Eucharist, you have the completeness of My love alive in you.

11/01/03 Jesus
The Eucharistic life is the best life anyone can live.

16/01/03 Jesus
I am the food of life,
I am the food of joy,
I am the food of eternity.
All those who will eat of Me in true love will have a joy-filled eternal life with Me in Heaven.

Jesus
All of heaven celebrates in every Eucharist and so should all of mankind.

17/01/03 Mother
The greatest gift God gives to you is His love in the Eucharist, which contains within it the fullness of His divinity and His humanity.

19/01/03 Mother
Let your life be fulfilled in my Son Jesus by filling yourself with Him in the Eucharist.

21/01/03 Jesus
Live My sacrifice every time you come to the Eucharist.

25/01/02 Father
In all of the world there are none closer to Me than those who unite in love with My Son Jesus in the Eucharist.

Romans 8:1 Those who are in Christ Jesus.

28/01/03 St Thomas Aquinas
Knowledge is not the greatest gift, the love of God in the Eucharist is!

01/02/03 Jesus
To exercise your soul, pray, fast, and read Holy Scripture.
To cleanse your soul, come to confession.
To fill your soul, come and unite with Me in the Eucharist.

15/02/03 Mother
Let the Eucharist lead you to true life by accepting my Son Jesus' presence within you without doubt and in love.

Amos 5:6 Seek the Lord that you may live.

04/03/03 Jesus
Take peoples' hearts to My heart by bringing them to Me in the Eucharist.

05/03/03 Mother
Holiness is found in God and God is found in the Eucharist and those who truly seek God will find Him there. Then they will find their way to holiness in His Eucharistic presence.

06/03/03 Jesus
In My Eucharistic presence is the power to overcome all disease.

07/03/03 Mother
With divine love in your heart when you receive my Son Jesus in the Eucharist, you should find your human love growing and your love of humanity increasing.

27/03/03 Jesus
The glory of My love can be found in every Eucharist and can be lived in every heart that receives Me in love.

02/04/03 Jesus
Find your life fulfilled in Me in every Eucharist.

03/04/03 Jesus
In adoration before Me your soul opens to be filled with My grace and to grow in My grace.

10/04/03 Jesus
As you receive Me you receive divine grace to help you grow more like Me.

11/04/03 Jesus
In My Eucharistic love there is a place for everyone.

19/04/03 Jesus
My body, My blood, given on the cross, received in the Eucharist.

14/05/03 Jesus
My grace abounds in every Catholic Church that contains My body and blood within it.

18/05/03 Jesus
My goodness flows into your heart in every Eucharist.

Psalms 34:9 Learn to savour how good the Lord is.

21/05/03 Father
To remain in My love remain in My Son Jesus in the Eucharist.

21/05/03 Jesus
Even though a spiritual union with Me is not as complete as uniting with Me in the Eucharist, it is still good to do so when you cannot receive My body, blood, soul and divinity in the Mass.

22/05/03 Jesus
All you seek, find in Me, in every Eucharist.

23/05/03 Mother
There is in every Eucharist the way to heaven for each person who will live in the Eucharist.

24/05/03 Jesus
A vision of loveliness,
A vision of beauty,
A vision of grace,
The vision of a soul filled with Me in the Eucharist.

Isaiah 18:7 The lord of hosts.

25/05/03 Jesus
The joy of love can be found in every Eucharist.

26/05/03 Jesus
Let your heart be strong in Me by placing your heart in Mine in every Eucharist.

30/05/03 Jesus
It is a love-filled gift - The Eucharist.

31/05/03 Mother
Going to Mass is going to God and going to His love for you.

31/05/03 Jesus
You grow in love in every Eucharist when you seek to be one in My love; one in Me.

05/06/03 Mother
The more you receive my Son in the Eucharist the more you grow in grace and love.

14/06/03 Jesus
It is in the Eucharist that you will find the way to truly love.

19/06/03 Jesus
In every Eucharist you can grow in holiness if you open yourself to Me and ask Me to help you be holy.

22/06/03 Father
Today as you eat and drink of My Son Jesus' body and blood think of how He gave His all for you so that you could become one in Him.

114.

22/06/03 Jesus
My body,
My blood,
My love for you.

22/06/03 Jesus
In every Eucharist My body and My blood wait to fill your entire being with My love.

30/06/03 Mother
To centre the day on the Eucharist makes the day complete.

13/07/03 Mother
With every day focusing on receiving my Son Jesus in the Eucharist you see more clearly the way life is meant to be.

Psalms 123:2 Our eyes are on the Lord our God.

13/07/03 Mother
In every heart that lives in the Eucharist is a fountain of grace filling not only that person, but the world around them.

Matthew 18:35 From his heart.

29/07/03 Jesus
The Eucharist is where all can see Me in My physical and Spiritual presence.

30/07/03 Jesus
While you are in My presence holiness surrounds you and fills you.

Ecclesiastes 5:1 In God's presence.

02/08/03 Jesus
The strength to do My will is within you because you receive that strength every time you receive Me in the Eucharist.

03/08/03 Jesus
A spirit can be renewed and refreshed by receiving Me in the Eucharist.

Wisdom 15:11 A vital spirit
Romans 8:11 His spirit that dwells in you.

03/08/03 Jesus
It does not matter in which language the Eucharist is celebrated, as the words remain Holy by the power of My Divine Spirit within them.

05/08/03 St Peter Julian
Eucharistic love is the love all Christians should have.

05/08/03 St Peter Julian
Within every Eucharist all the needs of mankind can be met and all it needs for this to happen is for mankind to come and meet the Lord Jesus in the Eucharist.

07/08/03 Jesus
In the Most Holy Sacrament of the Eucharist you will find the Most Holy, for you will find Me.

Tobit 8:15 Holy and pure.

13/08/03 Jesus
Just as you rest your body, you must rest your soul and you can do this by spending time alone with Me where My body and blood, My soul and My divinity are present and waiting to refresh you.

14/08/03 Father
The best time of the day is the time you receive My Son Jesus in the Eucharist.

15/08/03 Jesus
Let no one disturb your peace by keeping yourself firmly planted in My body and blood, soul and divinity in the Eucharist.

19/08/03 Father
Putting the Eucharist first in every day brings that day into its correct order.

19/08/03 Jesus
Eating My body and drinking My blood brings a soul to fullness in Me and should bring a life to fullness as well, if I am accepted completely within and not denied at all.

31/08/03 Mother
To truly experience the Eucharist, a person must immerse themselves in the Sacrament.

31/08/03 Jesus
Your love of the Eucharist shows your love of Me.

07/09/03 Jesus
If the Eucharist is the centre of your life, heaven is yours.

07/09/03 Jesus
The Eucharist is the holiest of the holy for it is Me.

Proverbs 21:2 It is the lord.

07/09/03 Jesus
The greatest celebration on earth is the Eucharist.

16/09/03 Jesus
Your heart dances in joy,
Your soul is filled with grace,
Your spirit is set on fire in Me in the Eucharist.

16/09/03 Jesus
Be at peace as My divinity unites your humanity with Me in the Eucharist.

28/09/03 Mother
The world cannot trap those who live in the Eucharistic love of my Son Jesus.

Romans 8:1 Those who are in Christ Jesus.

02/10/03 Mother
Enjoy the Mass by going to it seeking joy and seeking love in my Son Jesus.

07/10/03 Father
The Eucharist, the way to Me through My Son Jesus in His love and in His being.

10/10/03 Jesus
In the Eucharist you can find divinity if you open your eyes, heart and soul to see.

John 7:36 Look for me.

17/10/03 Mother
Through me in my Son Jesus all mankind became one in His flesh and for this oneness to achieve fullness, all people need to unite with His body and blood in the Eucharist.

17/10/03 Holy Spirit
In the Eucharist I fill your spirit with My spirit.

21/10/03 Jesus
In My Eucharistic heart there is a place for everyone.

25/10/03 Jesus
The richness of My love,
The treasure of My grace,
The wealth of My mercy...
The Eucharist.

26/10/03 Jesus
Let My love wash over and through you in every Eucharist.

26/10/03 Jesus
Let love lift you into My heart; the love of Me in the Eucharist.

Psalms 119:2 Who seek the Lord with all their heart.

28/10/03 St Simon the Apostle
God came to earth as man and I, as an apostle was blessed to see Him, to live with Him and to learn to love through Him.
Today God still comes to earth physically and spiritually in every Eucharist and all who believe this and live this will be blessed by His love as each one comes to find their body and soul united in Him.

29/10/03 Father
It is good to centre your day around the Eucharist.

29/10/03 Jesus
Those who desire to be one with Me should come to the Eucharist because in the Eucharist they can be.

03/11/03 Mother
Every Eucharist is a feast of love.

05/11/03 Jesus
The more people unite with Me in the Eucharist the more My peace and love will reside in their hearts.

10/11/03 Jesus
In the heart of every priest should be love of the Eucharist.

20/11/03 Jesus
In the Eucharist place your heart and find it filled with My love.

23/11/03 Jesus
In every Eucharist everyone who receives Me is touched by the divine to lift each one to greater heights of love and life.

24/11/03 Father
Every Mass you attend is full of My Son's loving grace for you.

24/11/03 Jesus
In every Eucharist every person should put their lives into Mine.

10/12/03 Jesus
It is in Me in the Eucharist you can find your true self and your true life.

14/12/03 Jesus
My body,
My blood,
My love for you.

18/12/03 Jesus
You will know My love in a deeper way by giving yourself totally to Me in the Eucharist.

20/12/03 Jesus
You are filled with grace when you receive Me in the Eucharist.

29/12/03 Jesus
As I am absorbed within by you when you receive Me in the Eucharist you too are absorbed into Me.

John 7:38 Within him.

13/01/04 Jesus
In My Divinity I lift your humanity on high when you unite with Me in the Eucharist.

24/01/04 Mother
You can grow in grace every day by receiving the Eucharist in love and by seeking grace in prayer and in all you do.

Psalms 25:1-2 I lift up my soul to my God.

25/01/04 Jesus
The Eucharist can bring you closer to Me if you will let it and if you desire it.

25/01/04 Jesus
The glory of My love can be seen by all if they look for it in the Eucharist.

11/02/04 Father
The Holy Mass can bring the masses to holiness.

13/02/04 Jesus
In every Eucharist your soul is fed with divine love so that it will have the strength to love as it should.

16/02/04 Jesus
Knowing My love in the Eucharist is the best way to know it.

21/02/04 Father
Let My Son Jesus' Eucharistic love guide you and fill you in every moment.

21/02/04 Jesus
In every Eucharist you can be changed to be more loving by Me and in Me.

03/03/04 Father
Enjoy the love of My Son Jesus in every Eucharist.

05/03/04 Jesus
You will find all the strength you need to live the way I ask in the Eucharist as it is here you will find Me.

07/03/04 Father
Within every Eucharist is all you need to live as I ask, for in each one is My Son Jesus waiting to guide you to a good life.

13/03/04 Jesus
My Kingdom can be found in every Eucharist.

Mark 9:1 The kingdom of God.

25/03/04 St Gabriel the Archangel
Every time you present yourself to God at the Eucharist, if you offer yourself to Him, you will grow in grace.

26/03/04 Jesus
In a union of love with Me all can grow in grace and grow in love.

28/03/04 Jesus
Your joy can be complete in Me by giving yourself completely to Me in each Eucharist.

28/03/04 Jesus
When doubt raises its ugly head come to the beauty of My love in the Eucharist and be filled with trust in Me.

31/03/04 Father
Go to the Eucharist joyfully and receive the divine joy of My Son Jesus' love so you can sustain your joy.

31/03/04 Jesus
Your heart can be like Mine if you give it to Me and allow Me to change it every time you come to unite with Me in the Eucharist.

06/04/04 Jesus
In union with Me you are united in love.

15/04/04 Jesus
True love can be found in every Eucharist as it is there My love can be found.

23/04/04 Jesus
I in you and you in Me when you give yourself to Me in the Eucharist.
United in love, united in My divinity and our humanity.
God and man…One, as it is meant to be.

24/04/04 Mother
The Holy Mass is always holy as long as the priest is truly ordained.

24/05/04 Jesus
Hearts of love, those truly united with Me in the Eucharist.

24/05/04 Jesus
I gave a Eucharistic Church so that all could live in Me.

28/05/04 Jesus
As a soul is united in My love in the Eucharist the heart of the person smiles with joy.

10/06/04 Jesus
In every Eucharist as people receive Me within they receive the doorway to heaven open wide for all who are prepared to open themselves in love to Me.

13/06/04 Jesus
In My body put your body.
In My blood put your blood.
In My soul put your soul.
In My divinity put your life and find your entire being filled with My divine presence.

13/06/04 Jesus
Living in the Eucharist is living in Me.

13/06/04 Jesus
The truth of the Eucharist is My truth.

13/06/04 Jesus
Every moment spent in My presence is a moment that you grow in grace.

13/06/04 Jesus
If you eat of My body and drink of My blood in love of Me, you then become more like Me.

13/06/04 Jesus
It is your faith to be Eucharistic.

16/06/04 Jesus
Many people do not know the love that resides in the Eucharist, help them know it!

Ezekiel 23:26 Make known to them
Isaiah 45:3 That I am the Lord.

20/06/04 Jesus
It is in the Eucharist that your faith can come alive.

06/07/04 Jesus
My love grows in your heart and soul every time you receive Me in the Eucharist.

07/07/04 Jesus
The mystery of My love is in the Eucharist.

10/07/04 Jesus
You become united in love in every Eucharist.

11/07/04 Jesus
You will never lose sight of My love if you keep seeking it in the Eucharist.

18/07/04 Jesus
As you give your heart and soul to Me in the Eucharist you open yourself wide to receive Me completely within.

20/07/04 Jesus
As you receive Me in the Eucharist not only am I absorbed into you but you are absorbed into Me. Then in this holy union I fill you with My love when you open yourself completely with the giving of your whole being to Me.

21/07/04 Jesus
To understand My love for you come to Me in the Eucharist and ask Me to show My love to you.

22/07/04 Jesus
Lift your heart into My love in every Eucharist.

26/07/04 Jesus
The more a person truly understands the Eucharist the more they realize they can never fully understand the greatest of the gifts I give.

27/07/04 Jesus
The divine moment of the Eucharist is an eternal moment.

28/07/04 Jesus
Every Mass, regardless of which language is used, is holy if it is celebrated by a truly ordained priest.

Ephesians 6:21 Trustworthy minister in the Lord.